to Mees Cornelis Hilarius
and Liv Isabel Victoria

M.T.

with thanks to my father

Jumping Penguins

MARIJE TOLMAN
with text by
JESSE GOOSSENS

Lemniscaat

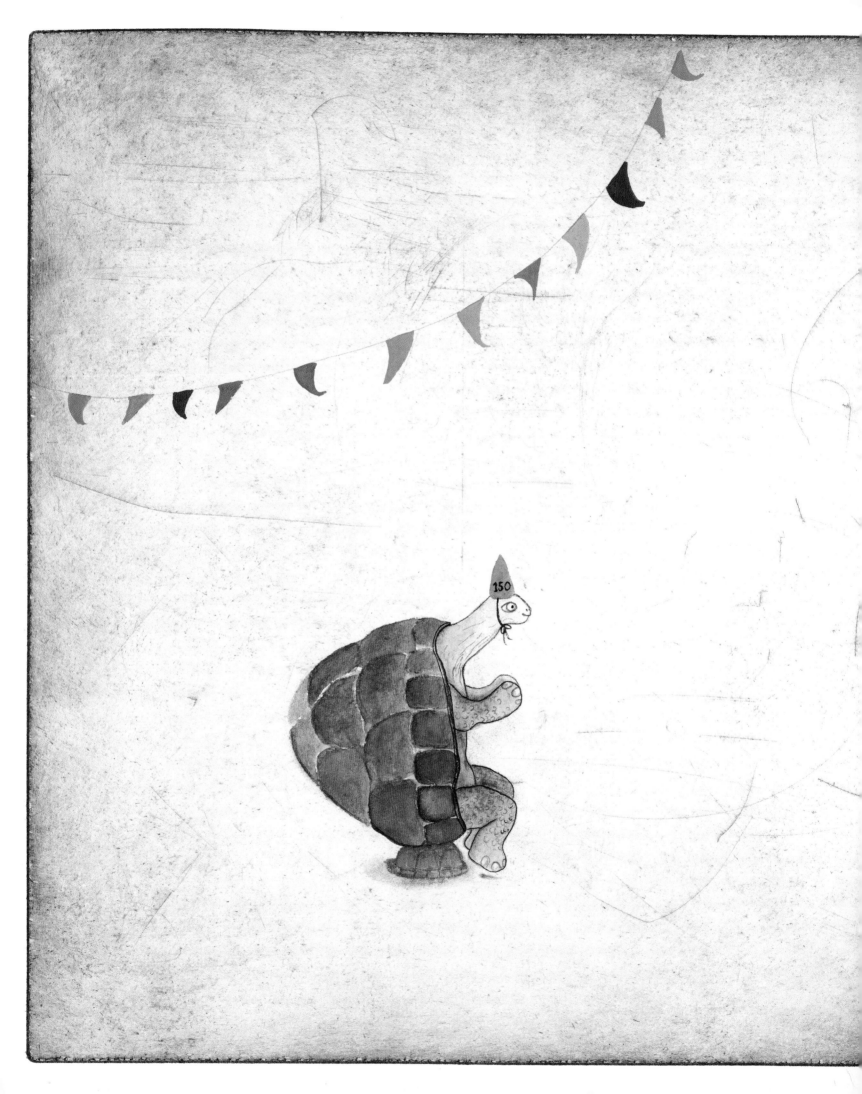

Turtle

There are about 330 species of turtles. The smallest is the speckled padloper tortoise that is between three and five inches long and weighs less than five ounces. The largest is the leatherback sea turtle which can be two meters long and weighs up to 2,000 pounds—as much as a small car.

Some species of turtles can live longer than 150 years. The oldest tortoise ever was an Aldabra giant tortoise called Adwaita that was at least 255 years old when it died.

Marabou

Marabous love wild fires. Once a marabou sees smoke or flames, it places itself in front of the fire in the path of animals escaping the heat. It selects the tastiest and eats them.

The legs of a marabou are dark gray or black but they look white because marabou storks always defecate on their own legs.
Its pink bald head and neck are often red from the blood of the carcasses it investigates.

Bison

A bison can weigh more than two tons and can jump six feet vertically and seven feet horizontally.

An angry bison can run 35 to 40 miles per hour.

Polar Bear

A polar bear is left-handed,
as are most artists.

Blue Whale

A blue whale weighs as much as thirty adult elephants. Its main artery is so large that a man could crawl through it.

A blue whale can eat up to 8,000 pounds of plankton per day, but it can also go without eating up to six months.

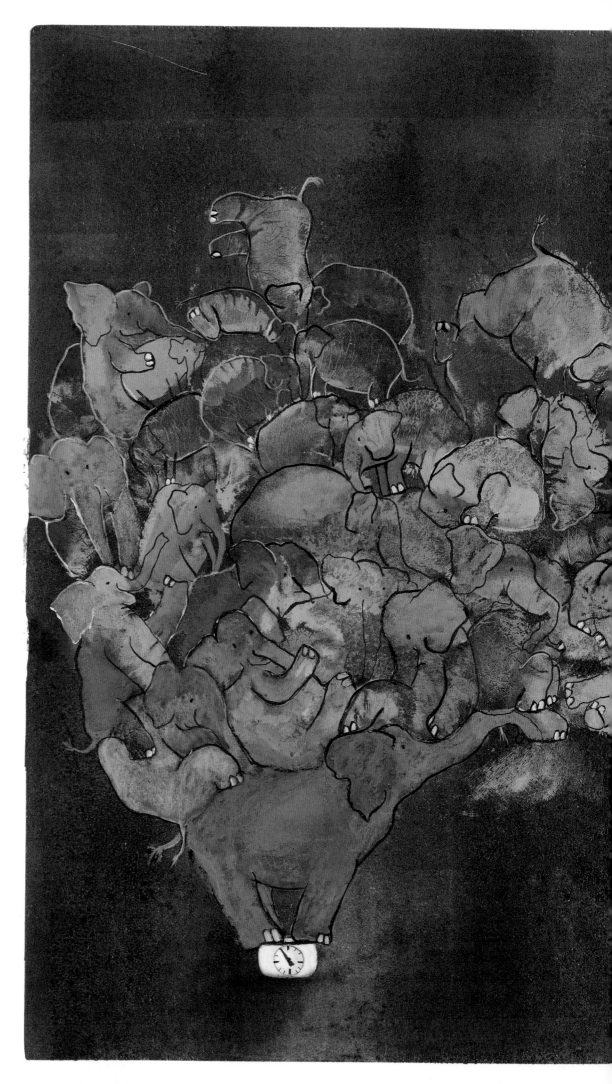

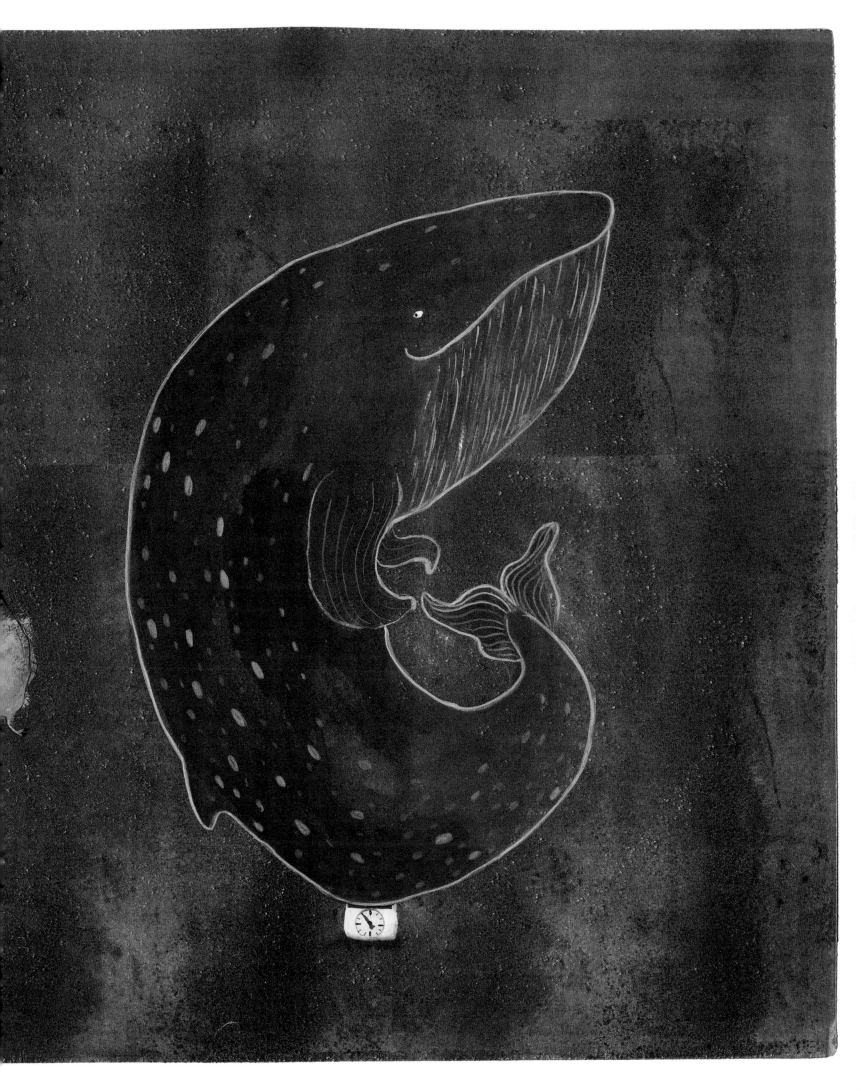

Flamingo

A flamingo feels safest when it has company. It prefers to be in a group with hundreds of its kind.

A flamingo gets its pink color from eating shrimp, other crustaceans, and algae. It can only eat if it swallows with its head upside down.

Seahorse

Who carries the babies? It is not the female but rather the male seahorse who has a pouch where the baby seahorses grow until it is time to be born. After birth, the male raises the seahorse babies. He gets pregnant again within a few days.

19

Giant Octopus

The biggest giant octopus ever found was over thirty feet long. However, a giant octopus can get through a hole as large as his own mouth. When a giant octopus is born, he is as small as a grain of rice.

The pupil of an octopus is rectangular. It has three hearts.

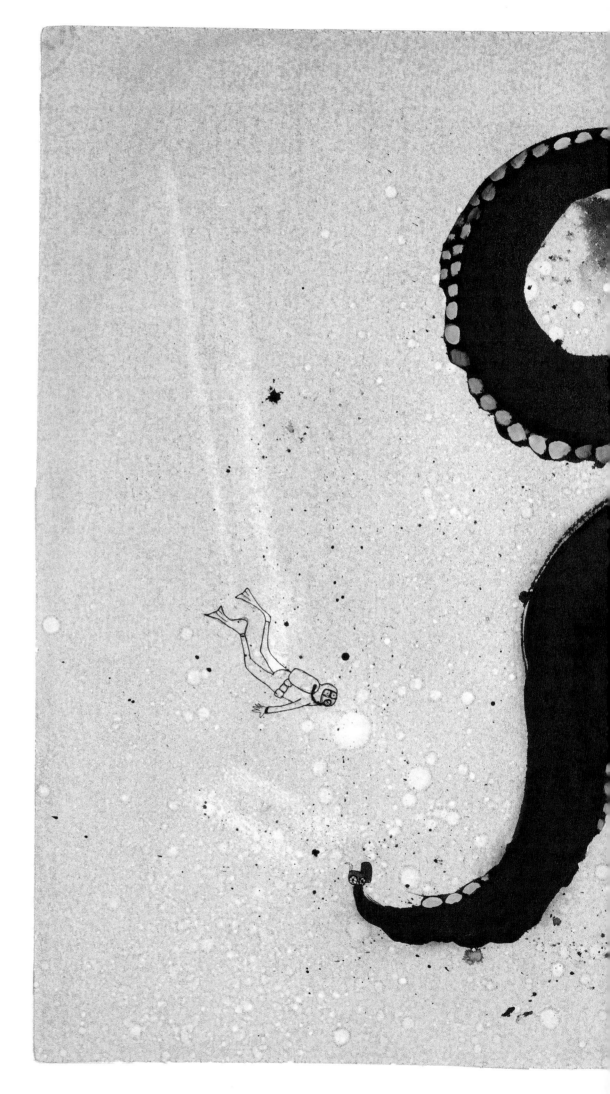

Giraffe

A giraffe has no vocal cords.
It has as many vertebrae as you
do.

Bat

A bat is the only mammal that can fly. It always flies to the left when leaving its cave.

The bones in the legs of a bat are so thin that it cannot stand on them.

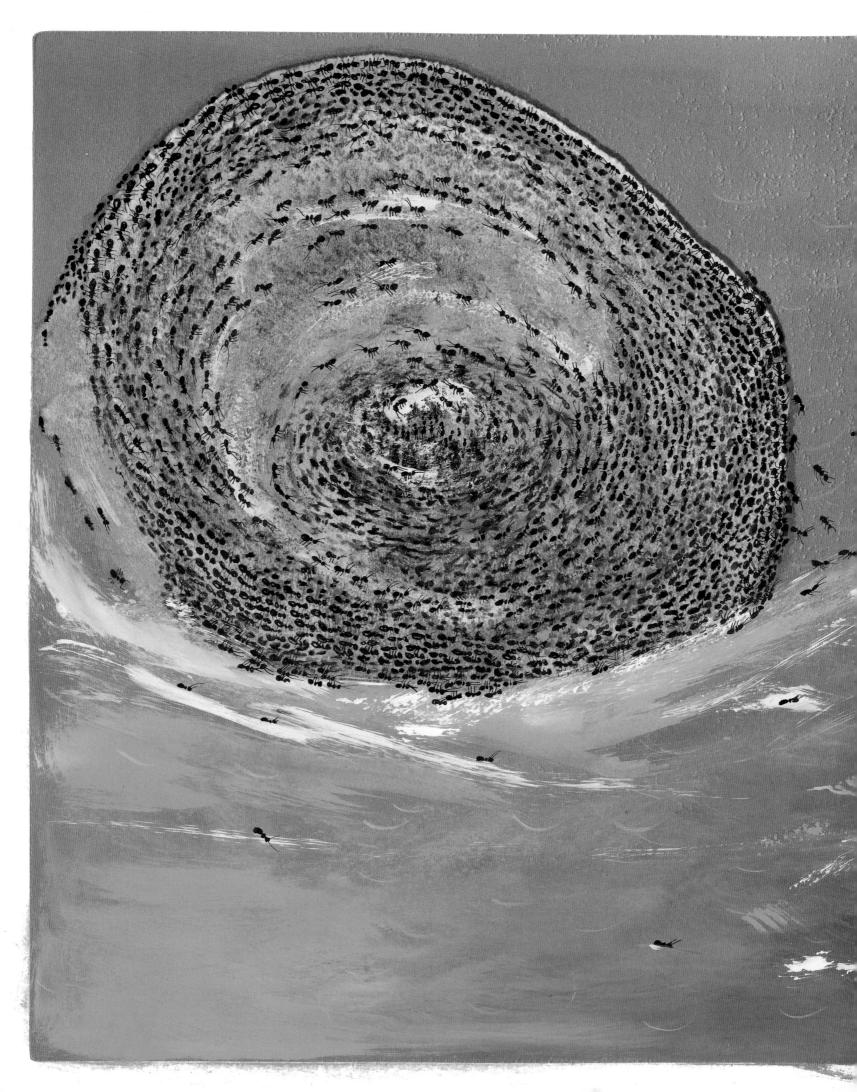

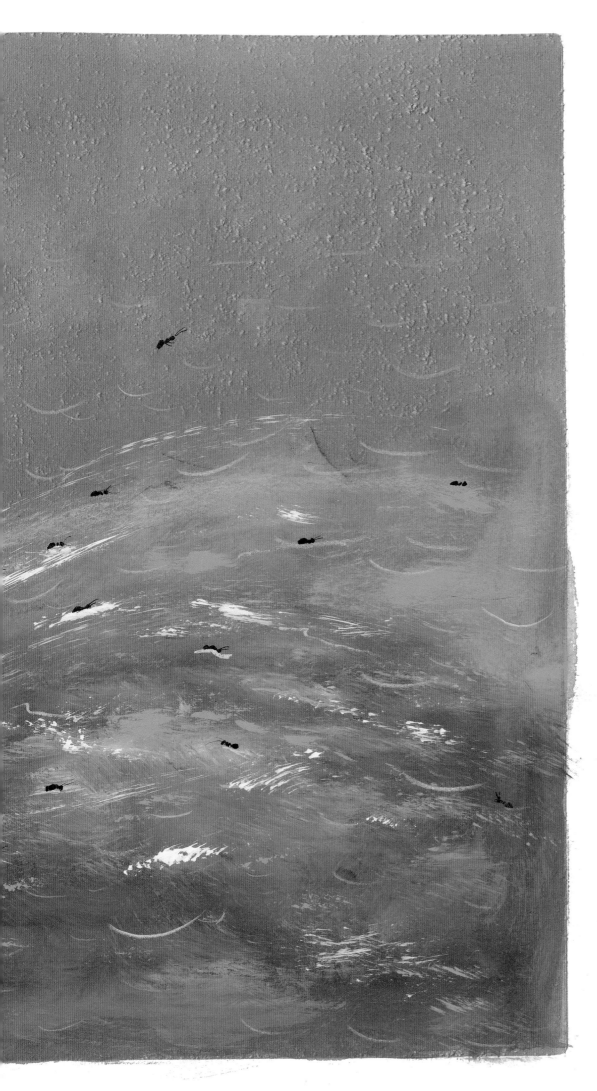

Ant

If tropical ants are hit by a flood, they roll up into a huge living ball that floats on the water. The young ants are safe and dry in the core.

Some species of ants can survive up to two weeks underwater.

Pelican

American White Pelicans fish in groups. They swim with four or five in a semicircle in the direction of the coast. With much flapping of wings and splashing, they drive the fish before them. Once they are in shallow water, the pelicans can easily catch the fish.

Gulls often sit on the head of a pelican to steal its fish when it opens its mouth to pour the water out.

Hippopotamus

The ribcage of a hippo is so huge that an average seven-year-old child could stand upright in its belly.

The eyes, nose, and ears of a hippopotamus are located on top of its head so that it can remain underwater longer.

Sloth

A sloth moves so slowly that green algae grows in its hair.

A sloth likes to be on its own. Once a week it comes out of its tree to defecate and urinate and meet other sloths.

There are sloths with two toes and there are sloths with three toes on its front paws. Two-toed sloths are bigger and can hang upside-down longer than three-toed sloths.

A sloth clings so tightly to its branch, it lingers even when it is dead.

Caterpillar

Some types of caterpillars can throw their poop extremely well. They throw their waste as far as possible so that the wasps —that would like to eat the caterpillars—cannot smell where they are. A caterpillar as big as a grain of rice can throw his poop 8 to 12 inches away that would be like a grown man throwing his poop between 100 and 130 feet.

Shark

Sharks have been around longer than dinosaurs. The oldest shark fossil is over 400 million years old.

A shark always keeps moving, even when it is sleeping.

The whale shark is the largest fish in the world. Its mouth has more than 4000 teeth but each tooth is less than a tenth of an inch and is not used. The whale shark's diet consists of small fish and plankton that it filters from the seawater.

Scorpion

Scorpions have six eyes and some even have twelve but they cannot see well. Scorpions have a complex mating dance—they grab each other by the pedipalps or pincers. After mating, the female sometimes consumes the male.

The first weeks of their life, young scorpions will ride on the backs of their mothers, but they are not completely safe. The mother will sometimes eat them if it is hungry enough.

If you drop some alcohol on a scorpion, it will go completely berserk and sting itself to death.

Crocodile

A crocodile really can cry but it does not cry because it is sad. A crocodile's tears wash the prickly salt from its eyes. This is why fake tears are called "crocodile tears."

A crocodile is a cannibal and will devour its relatives if it is hungry. Crocodiles are not picky eaters. Many large crocodiles will even eat stones that provide weight so the crocodile can stay under water. The stones also help grind the food in their stomachs.

Chameleon

A chameleon can rotate its eyes independently so it can look anywhere without turning its head. Even a blind chameleon will take on the color of its environment—it learns to recognize colors by smell and touch.

Panda

A giant panda has no permanent resting place. It just lies on the ground whenever it gets tired.

A panda has more colors than you might expect—its skin is black under its white coat and pink under its black coat.

Penguin

A penguin can launch itself from the water onto the land by jumping up to six feet high.

Penguins have been around for sixty million years. Early penguins were almost six feet tall.

Porcupine

Porcupines are nocturnal animals.

An adult porcupine has approximately 30,000 quills on its body which are replaced every year.

Wolf

A hungry wolf can eat up to 45 pounds of meat at once. This is comparable to a ten-year-old child eating 36 pounds of steak or 140 burgers at a single meal.

Lion

A male lion can sleep up to twenty hours a day. While the male rests, the females hunt, catching up to 90% of the food for the pride.

Tiger

Most cats do not like water, but tigers love it. The Sumatran tiger has webbed toes and can swim more than fifteen miles.

The teeth of a beaver jut out from its closed mouth so that it can work below the surface without breathing in water. It can shut its ears and eyes before it descends.

A beaver's teeth never stop growing. It keeps them at the correct length by gnawing.

Panther

A black panther is not a panther at all—it is a leopard that happens to be black.

First published in the United States and Canada in 2013
by Lemniscaat USA LLC · New York
Distributed in the United States by Lemniscaat USA LLC · New York

Cataloging-in-Publication Data is available.
ISBN 13: 978-1-935954-32-3 (Hardcover)
Printing and binding: Worzalla, Stevens Point, WI USA
First U.S. edition

Index